Everyday Food

Potatoes

Joyce Bentley

Chrysalis Children's Books

First published in the UK in 2005 by
Chrysalis Children's Books
An imprint of Chrysalis Books Group Plc
The Chrysalis Building, Bramley Road, London W10 6SP

ISBN 1 84458 183 7

British Library Cataloguing in Publication Data
for this book is available from the British Library.

Senior editor *Rasha Elsaeed*
Project editor *Debbie Foy*
Editorial assistant *Camilla Lloyd*
Food consultant *Brenda Alden*
Art director *Sarah Goodwin*
Illustrator *Molly Sage*
Designer *Ben Ruocco, Tall Tree Ltd*
Picture researchers *Sarah Stewart-Richardson, Veneta Bullen, Miguel Lamas*

Printed in China

10 9 8 7 6 5 4 3 2 1

Words in **bold** can be found in Words to remember on page 30.

Typography *Natascha Frensch*
Read Regular, READ SMALLCAPS and Read Space; European Community Design Registration 2003
and Copyright © Natascha Frensch 2001-2004 Read Medium, **Read Black** and *Read Slanted*
Copyright © Natascha Frensch 2003-2004

READ™ is a revolutionary new typeface that will enhance children's understanding through clear, easily
recognisable character shapes. With its evenly spaced and carefully designed characters, READ™ will help
children at all stages to improve their literacy skills, and is ideal for young readers, reluctant readers and
especially children with dyslexia.

Picture Acknowledgements
All reasonable efforts have been made to ensure the reproduction of content has been done with the consent
of copyright owners. If you are aware of any unintentional omissions please contact the publishers directly so
that any necessary corrections may be made for future editions.

Anthony Blake Photo Library: Graham Kirk 9T, Sian Irvine 1, 20, Norman Hollands 21B, Trevor Wood 23B;
British Potato Council: 9B, 17, 19; Bubbles Photo Library: Jennie Woodcock 26; Chrysalis Image Library: 23,
Ray Moller 24T, 24B, 25; Corbis: 7, ©Bettmann 6, Owen Franken 15, Gail Mooney BC, 18, Bennett Dean/Eye
Ubiquitous 22; Frank Lane Picture Agency: Desmond Dugan FC, 8, Mike J Thomas 10L, Peter Dean 10R, E & D
Hosking 16; Holt Studios: Nigel Cattlin 11, 12, 13, 14, 21T; Powerstock: Nils-Johan Norenlind 27; Royalty Free:
©Stockbyte 4; Science Photo Library: David Frazier/AGStock 5.

Contents

What are potatoes?

A potato is part of a plant that we can eat. It belongs to a group of foods called vegetables.

A potato is made up of a type of **carbohydrate**, called **starch**, and water.

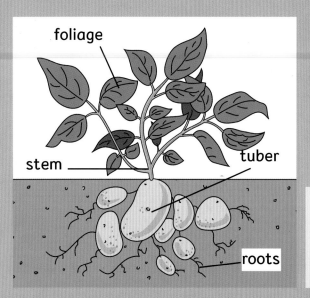

foliage

stem

tuber

roots

A potato plant showing the tuber and **foliage**.

Potatoes grow in soil under the ground.
Another name for the potato is the **tuber**.

The potato plant is pulled out of the ground with the tuber, foliage and roots attached.

Back in time

Potatoes were first grown by the Inca people over 600 years ago in the Andes mountains of Peru, South America.

This early drawing shows the Incas **harvesting** potatoes.

In 1845, the Irish potato **crop** failed and many people died of **starvation**. This was known as the Irish Potato Famine.

When the Spanish **invaded** Peru, they brought potatoes back with them and they soon became popular in Europe. They first arrived in Virginia, USA, in 1621.

There are over 100 different types of potato!

All sorts of potatoes

Potatoes come in many varieties such as King Edward's, Maris Piper and Jersey. They can be many different shapes, sizes and colours.

Potatoes can be brown, green, yellow, red and purple.

Potatoes are described as waxy or floury. Waxy potatoes stay firm when cooked and keep their shape. Floury potatoes crumble easily when cooked.

Floury potatoes are ideal for mashing.

Waxy potatoes are good for covering stews and casseroles or serving on their own.

9

Planting potatoes

Potatoes grow from **seed potatoes**.
Before the seeds are planted, the farmer
uses a tractor to pull the **plough**. This
prepares the soil for planting.

A machine
called a planter
sows the seed
potatoes in rows.

The plough
has sharp blades
that turn the soil
over as they
move.

When the soil is ready, a machine plants the seeds. It makes **grooves** in the soil as it drops the seed potatoes into the ground.

Seed potatoes are potatoes that have grown new **shoots** and, when sown, will grow into potato plants.

Growing potatoes

After planting, the potatoes are left to grow. They need sunlight and water to reach their full size.

Fertilisers are being sprayed onto these potato plants to help them grow.

Potatoes will not grow if there is a **drought**. The potato crop must be protected from threats, such as disease and pests, and may have to be watered if there is no rain.

Potatoes were the first vegetables to be grown in Space!

Slugs and **blight** are common threats to potatoes. The may damage the potato plant.

Potato seasons

There are two potato seasons a year.
New potatoes are planted in March
and harvested from April to June.

Potatoes grow best in direct sunlight and are planted north to south so that the whole plant sees the sun.

Mid-crop potatoes are planted in April and harvested in September.

Potatoes were eaten during World War I and II, as food was in short supply and they were easy to grow.

Potatoes take 13 to 17 weeks to grow.

Harvest time

Harvesting is when a crop is pulled
from the ground to be eaten. Chemicals
are sprayed onto the foliage to kill it,
leaving the potato behind.

The harvester shakes the potatoes to remove any loose soil.

A machine called a harvester lifts the potatoes out of the ground. It also separates the potato from the soil and any dead foliage.

Some potatoes have hairs on their leaves to protect them from frost and blight.

Potatoes are stored in a warehouse before being sent to the shops or factory.

Getting to you

Farm workers check the potatoes and remove any **rotten** ones. They are packed into sacks or crates ready for transporting to supermarkets and shops.

Farm workers in France are checking the potatoes as they are harvested.

Some potatoes are packed into plastic bags in factories or sold loose in crates. You can also buy sacks of potatoes direct from the farmer.

Potatoes are called 'spuds' after the spade that was used to dig them up.

Potatoes are often sold in plastic bags showing their **sell-by-date**.

Eating potatoes

Potatoes need to be cooked before they can be eaten. You can boil, bake, mash, chip, fry, **sauté**, roast or steam them.

These potatoes have been sautéed in hot oil with herbs and may be served as a side dish.

Crisps are thinly sliced, deep fried potatoes. They come in many flavours.

Potatoes are ideal as part of a dish, either with toppings and fillings or simply with a knob of butter.

Bake jacket potatoes for about an hour and then fill them with cheese, tinned fish or vegetables.

Everyone loves potatoes

Potatoes are enjoyed around the world. They form part of a **staple diet** for many people as they are cheap and easily available.

Potato curry is a traditional dish in many parts of India.

22

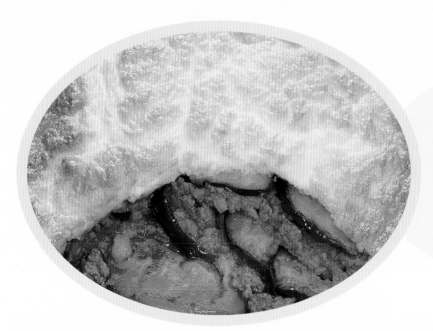

Moussaka comes from Greece. It is made with layers of **aubergine**, minced meat and potato.

Many countries have their own special potato recipes made with other locally grown **produce**.

Latkes, or potato cakes, are eaten during the Jewish festival of **Chanukkah**.

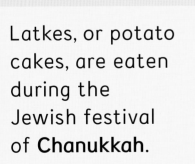

A balanced diet

Potatoes are a carbohydrate. They are rich in **fibre** and **vitamins**. We need these nutrients as part of a balanced diet.

Other carbohydrates include pasta, bread and rice.

Fruit and vegetables are carbohydrates that also provide lots of vitamins and fibre.

For a balanced diet, most of the food we eat should come from the groups at the bottom of the chart and less from the top.

Fat, oils and sweets group

Milk group

Meat group, *including fish, nuts and eggs*

Vegetable group

Fruit group

Grain group, *including potatoes*

Healthy potatoes

We need carbohydrates to give us energy. Fibre is essential to our diet as it helps our food to digest properly.

Children need lots of carbohydrates as they are usually more active than adults.

Vitamins give us healthy hair, skin and nails. They also help to prevent us from becoming ill.

Potatoes contain almost no fat at all!

Athletes eat carbohydrates when they are training.

Potato boats

Turn jacket potatoes into boats by adding a few ingredients. Your boats can also float on spaghetti shapes!
Serves 2

YOU WILL NEED

- 2 baking potatoes, washed
- 1 oz/25g butter
- Small tin of baked beans
- 2 oz/50g cheese
- Cocktail sticks

1. Preheat the oven to 200°C /400°F/ gas mark 6. Prick the potatoes with a fork and bake them for one hour.

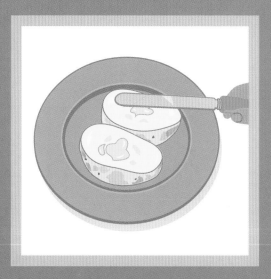

2. Allow the potatoes to cool, then cut them in half. Place them on plates with the flat side facing up. Add the butter to the potato halves.

3. Heat the beans and pour them onto the plate around the potatoes to make a baked bean 'sea'.

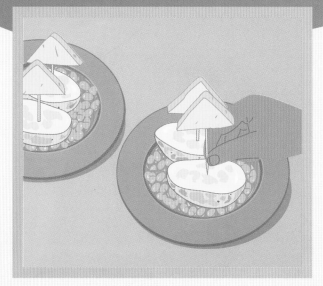

4. Cut out some triangles of cheese and place them on cocktail sticks. Stick them into the potato boats to make 'sails'.

aubergine Dark purple, pear-shaped vegetable.

blight Disease that affects plants.

carbohydrate Nutrient the body needs for energy.

Chanukkah The Jewish 'Festival of Lights'.

crop Plants that are grown for food.

drought Long periods with no rain.

fertiliser Chemical that kill pests and disease.

fibre Material found in plants and grains that helps digestion.

foliage The leaves, flowers and pods of a plant.

grooves A deep line cut into a flat surface.

harvesting To pull a crop from the ground when it is ready to eat.

invaded When something is attacked and damaged.

mid-crop Potatoes are planted twice a year. Mid-crop potatoes are the second planting.

new potatoes Young potatoes.

pests Insects that damage crops.

plough Machine that turns over the soil ready for planting.

produce Food that is grown to sell.

rotten When something is no longer fit to eat.

sauté To cook quickly in a small amount of oil.

seed potatoes Potatoes that have shoots and, when planted, will grow into potato plants.

sell-by-date The date by which something should be sold.

shoots The first stems that will go on to become fully grown plants.

sow To place seeds in the ground so they will grow into plants.

staple diet Food that forms the main part of the diet.

starch A kind of carbohydrate.

starvation When people have no food to eat their bodies cannot work and they may die.

tuber Part of the potato plant that grows underground and that we eat.

vitamins Nutrients the body needs for good health and to prevent illness.

Index